Primary Mathematics: Audit and Test
Assessing your knowledge and understanding

Second edition

Claire Mooney
Mike Fletcher

Learning Matters

First published in 2001 by Learning Matters Ltd.
Reprinted in 2002.
Second edition published in 2003.

British Library Cataloguing in Publication Data
A CIP record for this book is available from the British Library.

ISBN 1 903300 87 8

Cover design by Topics – The Creative Partnership
Text design by Code 5 Design Associates Ltd
Project Management by Deer Park Productions
Typeset and illustrated by PDQ Typesetting
Printed and bound in Great Britain by The Baskerville Press Ltd, Salisbury, Wiltshire.

Learning Matters Ltd
33 Southernhay East
Exeter EX1 1NX
Tel: 01392 215560
Email: info@learningmatters.co.uk
www.learningmatters.co.uk

Contents

Introduction   1

Part 1: Mathematics background   4

Part 2: Interest in mathematics   5

Part 3: Perceived competence and confidence in mathematics   6
    Competence   6
       Making sense of your perceived competence   8
    Confidence   9
       Making sense of your perceived confidence   10

Part 4: Mathematics test   11
    Number   11
    Algebra – patterns and relationships   14
    Shape and space   16
    Statistics   22
    Probability   22
    Measures   23
    Equations and graphs   24
    Reasoning and proof   26
    Making sense of your test results   26

Part 5: Answers to test questions   28

Part 6: Targets for further development   41

Part 7: Suggestions for revision and further reading   42

About this book

This book has been written to support the subject knowledge learning of all primary trainee teachers on all courses of Initial Teacher Training (ITT) in England and other parts of the UK where a secure subject knowledge and understanding of mathematics is required for the award of Qualified Teacher Status (QTS). A secure subject knowledge and understanding of mathematics is now widely acknowledged as a critical factor at every point in the complex process of planning, teaching and assessing mathematics itself. The audit and test materials presented here in seven parts are intended to help you to identify your own strengths and weaknesses in mathematics and to help you to set clear, appropriate and achievable targets for your own mathematical development:

→ *Part 1: Mathematics background;*

→ *Part 2: Interest in mathematics;*

→ *Part 3: Perceived competence and confidence in mathematics;*

→ *Part 4: Mathematics test;*

→ *Part 5: Answers;*

→ *Part 6: Targets for further development;*

→ *Part 7: Suggestions for revision and further reading.*

It is quite likely that you will be required to undertake further auditing and testing of your subject knowledge and understanding of mathematics at the start of your own course of ITT. You may wish to retain the audit and test results here for your own records and use them as working documents to return to as and when necessary. Your ITT provider may also wish to use them for their records too.

You may indeed find the auditing and testing of your mathematics subject knowledge a daunting prospect, especially if you have not studied mathematics for several years. However, most people simply take it all in their stride and you should aim to do the same. Undertaking a self-audit and testing your own mathematical knowledge is just one part of the assessment process you will experience both during training and throughout your career in teaching. There is certainly nothing to worry about when auditing and testing yourself in the comfort of your own home, and your ITT provider will take every step it can to help you towards your goal of becoming an effective and successful primary school teacher.

For trainees wishing to undertake some revision or who feel the need for a mathematics study aid there are several excellent books written specifically for primary trainees with diverse backgrounds in mathematics, all available from good booksellers. The *Learning Matters QTS Series* includes *Primary Mathematics: Knowledge and Understanding* (second edition) by Mooney et al. (full details in References). Additional ideas for revision and further study are included in Part 7.

The Professional Standards for Qualified Teacher Status

Qualifying to Teach (DfES/TTA 2002) provides the statutory framework for Initial Teacher Training. It specifies both the Professional Standards which trainee teachers must meet if they are to be awarded

QTS, and the requirements for ITT providers. It includes the requirement that all primary trainees on all courses of Initial Teacher Training must, when assessed, demonstrate that they have a secure knowledge and understanding of the subject content of mathematics. Where gaps in subject knowledge and understanding are identified, ITT providers are required to ensure that those areas needing attention are addressed and that, by the end of their course, trainees are both competent and confident in using their knowledge and understanding of mathematics in their teaching. An appropriate subject content for mathematics includes:

→ *the real number system;*

→ *indices;*

→ *number operations and algebra;*

→ *equations, functions and graphs;*

→ *mathematical reasoning and proof;*

→ *measures;*

→ *shape and space;*

→ *probability and statistics.*

The self-audit and test materials presented here will introduce you to the content items listed above in detail.

Mathematics: the National Curriculum for England

So just what is it that all of this subject knowledge and understanding supports? In 1989, all maintained schools throughout England and Wales experienced the introduction of a National Curriculum for Mathematics. Mathematics in the National Curriculum is organised on the basis of four Key Stages of which Key Stage 1 for 5- to 7-year-olds (Years 1 and 2) and Key Stage 2 for 7- to 11-year-olds (Years 3 to 6) are for primary. The components of each Key Stage include Programmes of Study, which set out the mathematics that children should be taught; Attainment Targets, which set out the mathematical knowledge, skills and understanding that children should attain; and Level Descriptions, which describe the types and range of performance that children working at a particular level should be able to demonstrate within each Attainment Target. A brief summary of Programmes of Study is presented as follows:

→ *Ma 1: Using and applying mathematics;*

→ *Ma 2: Number and algebra;*

→ *Ma 3: Shape, space and measures;*

→ *Ma 4: Handling data (Key Stage 2).*

The statutory Mathematics National Curriculum is now supported by the National Numeracy Strategy's *Framework for Teaching Mathematics* (non-statutory).

References

DfEE/QCA (1999) *Mathematics: the National Curriculum for England*. London: HMSO. (Also available online at *http://www.nc.uk.net*.)

DfEE (1999) *The National Numeracy Strategy: Framework for Teaching Mathematics*. London: DfEE. (Also available online at *http://www.standards.dfee.gov.uk/numeracy/NNSframework/*.)

Mooney, C. et al. (2002) *Primary Mathematics: Knowledge and Understanding*. (2nd ed.) Exeter: Learning Matters.

DfES/TTA (2002) *Qualifying to Teach: Professional Standards for Qualified Teacher Status and Requirements for Initial Teacher Training*. London: TTA. (Also available online at www.canteach.gov.uk)

Part 1: Mathematics background

Provide as many background details as you can. Don't worry if it looks a bit 'blank' in places, you won't be alone.

→ *personal details*

Name

Date of birth

Year(s) of course

Subject specialism

Elected Key Stage

→ mathematics qualifications

GCSE/O level (equivalent)

Date taken

Grade(s)

GCE A level (equivalent)

Date taken

Grade(s)

→ mathematics degree

Year of graduation

Class of degree

Other mathematics courses

→ other *(e.g. work related)*

A positive attitude towards mathematics will help you to learn and teach it well, whether it is your favourite subject or not. Be honest with yourself and think carefully about your responses below. It is possible that you might have a healthy interest in mathematics even if you currently think you don't know much about it, and unfortunately the converse might be true!

Circle as appropriate using the key provided.

1 = *I am very interested in mathematics.*
2 = *I am interested in mathematics.*
3 = *I am uncertain about my interest in mathematics.*
4 = *I am not interested in mathematics.*

→ **Interest**   **1**   **2**   **3**   **4**

A **1** or a **2** is fantastic, a **3** encouraging, a **4** – well, you have yet to be inspired! Reflect critically on your attitude towards mathematics, positive or negative, and use the space below to comment further. Can you identify the experiences that gave rise to your interest or lack of interest in mathematics?

→ ***experiences statement***

As you undertake the following self-audit you might notice that you feel quite competent in an area of mathematics but lack the confidence to teach it. Competence and confidence are clearly quite different things. By the end of your training you will have greater competence within mathematics and greater confidence to teach the subject.

Competence

There are rather a lot of areas within this self-audit and you will need some time to read through and complete this part thoroughly. You do not need to know about or feel competent with everything listed here right now. This will develop throughout your training.

Please respond to the following statements using the key provided.

1 = Very good. Existing competence perceived as exceeding the requirements.

2 = Good. Existing competence perceived as meeting the requirements comfortably.

3 = Adequate. Existing competence perceived as meeting the requirements but some uncertainties still exist.

4 = Not good. Existing competence perceived as not meeting the requirements.

Number and algebra

	1	2	3	4
a) the real number system				
• the arithmetic of integers, fractions and decimals	○	○	○	○
• forming equalities and inequalities and recognising when equality is preserved	○	○	○	○
• the distinction between a rational number and an irrational number making sense of simple recurring decimals	○	○	○	○
b) indices				
• representing numbers in index form including positive and negative integer exponents	○	○	○	○
• standard form	○	○	○	○
c) number operations and algebra				
• using the associative, commutative and distributive laws	○	○	○	○
• use of cancellation to simplify calculations	○	○	○	○
• using the multiplicative structure of ratio and proportion to solve problems	○	○	○	○

- finding factors and multiples of numbers and of simple algebraic expressions
- constructing general statements
- manipulating simple algebraic expressions and using formulae
- knowing when numerical expressions and algebraic expressions are equivalent
- number sequences, their *nth* terms and their sums

d) equations, functions and graphs

- forming equations and solving linear and simultaneous linear equations, finding exact solutions
- interpreting functions and finding inverses of simple functions
- representing functions graphically and algebraically
- understanding the significance of gradients and intercepts
- interpreting graphs, and using them to solve equations

Mathematical reasoning and proof

	1	2	3	4

- the correct use of =, ≡, ⇒, ∴
- the difference between mathematical reasoning and explanation, as well as the proper use of evidence
- following rigorous mathematical argument
- familiarity with methods of proof, including simple deductive proof, proof by exhaustion and disproof by counter-example

Measures

	1	2	3	4

- understanding that the basis of measures is exact and that practical measurement is approximate
- standard measures and compound measures, including rates of change
- the relationship between measures, including length, area, volume and capacity
- understanding the importance of choice of unit and use of proportion

Shape and space

	1	2	3	4

- Cartesian coordinates in 2-D
- 2-D transformations
- angles, congruence and similarity in triangles and other shapes
- geometrical constructions
- identifying and measuring properties and characteristics of 2-D shapes
- using Pythagoras' theorem

7

- recognising the relationships between and using the formulae for the area of 2-D shapes; including rectangle and triangle, trapezium, and parallelogram
- the calculation of the area of circles and sectors, the length of circumferences and arcs
- recognise, understand and use formulae for the surface area and volume of prisms
- identifying 3-D solids and shapes and recognising their properties and characteristics

Probability and statistics

1   2   3   4

- using discrete and continuous data and understanding the difference between them
- tabulating and representing data diagrammatically and graphically
- interpreting data and predicting from data
- finding and using the mean and other central measures
- finding and using measures of spread to compare distributions
- using systematic methods for identifying, counting and organising events and outcomes
- understanding the difference between probability and observed relative frequencies
- recognise independent and mutually exclusive events

Making sense of your perceived competence

Look back over the **perceived competency** grades within your self-audit. Summarise each area in the following table by looking at the distribution of responses. For example, if you ticked **1**s, **2**s and **3**s in *The real number system* but no **4**s, you should fill in your Range as **1**s to **3**s. If you ticked more **3**s than anything else, you should fill in your Mode, the most frequently occurring response, as **3**.

	range	mode
The real number system		
Indices		
Number operations and algebra		
Equations, functions and graphs		
Mathematical reasoning and proof		
Measures		
Shape and space		
Probability and statistics		

Mostly 1s   Areas summarised as mostly 1s suggest that most competency requirements are exceeded. Your perceived competence would place you at a level beyond that indicated for a non-mathematics specialist. Well done.

Mostly 2s   Areas summarised as mostly 2s suggest that most competency requirements are met comfortably. Some attention is necessary locally, certainly in weaker elements. Your perceived competence places you at a level about that of a non-mathematics specialist. With this sort of profile you probably have little to worry about.

Mostly 3s   Areas summarised as mostly 3s suggest that most competency requirements are met adequately. However, attention is necessary throughout. Your perceived competence places you at a level best described as approaching that specified for a non-mathematics specialist. You are probably in good company and with a little effort you will be up there with the best of them.

Mostly 4s   Areas summarised as mostly 4s suggest that most competency requirements are hardly being met at all, but remember, you only have to get there by the end of your training – not before! Given the nature of the subject knowledge, a profile like this is not surprising. Consistent effort throughout your training will certainly result in a much improved competency profile, so don't worry.

Confidence

Carefully examine the Programmes of Study for Key Stages 1 and 2 in the Mathematics National Curriculum given below. Overall, how would you describe your confidence in terms of **teaching** them? Respond using the key provided.

1 = Very good. Might even feel happy to support colleagues!

2 = Good. Further professional development required in some aspects.

3 = Adequate. Further professional development required in most aspects.

4 = Poor. Help! Further professional development essential in all aspects.

Ma2: Number

	1	2	3	4
using and applying number	◯	◯	◯	◯
numbers and the number system	◯	◯	◯	◯
calculations	◯	◯	◯	◯
solving numerical problems	◯	◯	◯	◯

Ma3: Shape, space and measures

	1	2	3	4
using and applying shape, space and measures	◯	◯	◯	◯
understanding patterns and properties of shape	◯	◯	◯	◯
understanding properties of position and movement	◯	◯	◯	◯
understanding measures	◯	◯	◯	◯

Ma4: Handling data (Key Stage 2)

- using and applying handling data
- processing, representing and interpreting data

Making sense of your perceived confidence

*1*s and *2*s are fantastic – what's kept you away from the profession for so long?! *3*s are encouraging and we would imagine many people would have this sort of profile. If you ticked any *4*s, don't worry, you are being honest with yourself and that is good. If you felt so confident about teaching mathematics at this stage, it would be difficult to convince you that there was any point in training you to do it! Reflect critically on your perceived confidence about teaching mathematics and use the space below to comment further. Can you identify the 'source' of your confidence or the 'source' of your lack of it?

→ **confidence statement**

$$45 \times 24$$

$$\begin{array}{r} 45 \\ \times\ 2\ 4 \\ \hline 1\ 8^2\ 0 \\ 9^1\ 0\ 0 \\ \hline 10\ 80 \end{array}$$

Perceived competence and confidence is one thing. How would you do if actually put to the test! It really doesn't matter how well or how badly you do in the test now, you have lots of time to make up for the mathematics you have forgotten or never knew in the first place. The following pages explore your knowledge and understanding in the areas of mathematics identified in the self-audit in Part 3. Take as long as you need and try not to cheat too much by looking at the answers! The marking system is quite straightforward and easy to use.

Number

❶ Using a method for long multiplication work out the following:

(i) 45×24 (ii) 146×234 (iii) 312×235

(3 marks)

❷ Use a long division algorithm to solve:

(i) $1768 \div 34$ (ii) $1638 \div 63$ (iii) $3335 \div 23$

(3 marks)

Key vocabulary: *algorithm, place value, operation, dividend, divisor, quotient*

❸ Using $p = \frac{2}{3}$, $q = \frac{1}{2}$, $r = 2\frac{4}{7}$ and $s = 1\frac{1}{5}$ find:

(i) $p + q$ (ii) $p + r$ (iii) $q + s$
(iv) $p - q$ (v) $r - q$ (vi) $r - s$
(vii) $p \times q$ (viii) $q \times s$ (ix) $r \times s$
(x) $p \div q$ (xi) $q \div p$ (xii) $q \div r$

(12 marks)

Key vocabulary: *fraction, numerator, denominator, proper fraction, improper fraction*

❹ Convert the following into decimal fractions:

(i) $\frac{5}{8}$ (ii) $\frac{7}{20}$ (iii) 65% (iv) 0.1%

(4 marks)

❺ Convert the following to vulgar fractions:

(i) 0.375 (ii) 0.28 (iii) 76%

(3 marks)

❻ Express the following fractions in their simplest forms:

(i) $\frac{84}{96}$ (ii) $\frac{84}{91}$

(2 marks)

❼ Convert the following into percentages:

(i) $\frac{5}{8}$ (ii) 0.375 (iii) $\frac{7}{20}$ (iv) 0.28

(4 marks)

> **Key vocabulary:** *equivalence, equivalent fraction, common denominator, vulgar fraction, decimal fraction*

8 Prior to Christmas the cost of the latest computer game was increased by 20%. In the sales after Christmas it was reduced by 20%. How do the two prices compare?

(1 mark)

9 As it was so desirable, the cost of the latest mobile phone was increased by 25%. A month later it was no longer fashionable and was reduced by 20%. How did the reduced price compare with the original price before the increase?

(1 mark)

10 A school basketball team scored 24 points in one game and 30 points in the next. What was their percentage increase in the points scored?

(1 mark)

11 Two children undertake a sponsored swim. In total they raise £160. The ratio of the contributions of Edward to Katherine was 2:3. How much did each child raise?

(2 marks)

12 A junior school shares out library books to year groups based on the ratio of the number of children in the year groups. 1000 books are to be distributed to Years 3, 4, 5 and 6. There are 52 children in Year 3, 68 in Year 4, 44 in Year 5 and 36 in Year 6. How many books does each year group get?

(4 marks)

> **Key vocabulary:** *percentage, ratio, proportion*

13 Place a tick in the box next to the numbers that are rational and a cross next to the numbers that are irrational.

(i) 0.3636363... ☐   (ii) $\sqrt{2}$ ☐   (iii) $\sqrt{4}$ ☐

(iv) 0.101001000100001... ☐   (v) $\frac{1}{9}$ ☐   (vi) $\sqrt{\frac{4}{9}}$ ☐

(vii) π ☐   (viii) 2^3 ☐   (ix) 2^{-3} ☐

(9 marks)

14 Place the numbers from question 13 in numerical order. Also include the following numbers:

$\frac{1}{7}$ $-\sqrt{5}$ $-(2^2)$ $-(2^{-2})$ $0.\dot{3}$

(7 marks)

15 0.33333... can be written as $0.\dot{3}$. Write the following recurring decimals using the same notation:

(i) 0.27272727...   (ii) 0.277777777...
(iii) 0.904904904904...   (iv) 18.18181818...

(4 marks)

> **Key vocabulary:** *rational number, irrational number, recurring decimal, real number*

⑯ Write these numbers in index form:

(i) 100 000   (ii) 0.1   (iii) 100

(3 marks)

⑰ Convert these numbers from standard form into ordinary form

(i) 6.6×10^3 (ii) 7.07×10^{-2}

(2 marks)

⑱ Write these numbers in standard form

(i) 523 000   (ii) 0.0606

(2 marks)

Key vocabulary: *index form, exponent, standard form*

⑲ Put a tick in the box if the statement is **true** and a cross if the statement is **false**.

(i) $(24 + 8) \div 4 = (24 \div 4) + (8 \div 4)$ ☐

(ii) $(96 \div 12) \div 4 = 96 \div (12 \div 4)$ ☐

(iii)   17% of £50 = 50% of £17   ☐

(iv) $(20 + 8) \times (30 + 9) = (20 \times 30) + (8 \times 9)$ ☐

(4 marks)

Key vocabulary: *commutative, associative, distributive, order of precedence, (BODMAS)*

⑳ Find all the factors of each of the following numbers:

(i)   18   (ii)   60

(2 marks)

㉑ Find all the prime factors of each of the following numbers:

(i)   48   (ii)   105

(2 marks)

㉒ Find the highest common factor of each of the following:

(i)   6 and 15   (ii)   18 and 54

(iii) $12a^2$ and $4ab$ (iv) a^2b and a^3b^2

(4 marks)

Key vocabulary: *factor, common factor, prime factor, multiple*

Algebra – patterns and relationships

1 If $a = 5$, $b = 15$, $c = 2$, $d = 3$, $de = 15$ and $df = 18$ find:

(i) ab (ii) ac (iii) e

(iv) f (v) $a(b + c)$ (vi) $d(e + f)$

(vii) $a(b - c)$ (viii) $d(e - f)$ (ix) $2a^2b$

(x) $2d^2e$ (xi) $\frac{1}{a}$ (xii) $\frac{1}{d}$

(12 marks)

2 Lydia is doing a mathematics investigation and obtains the results 1, 4, 9, 16, 25.

(i)   What would be the next term in this sequence?

(1 mark)

(ii)   The 10th term?

(1 mark)

(iii) The nth term?

(2 marks)

3 Tom is investigating the number of slabs that would be required to pave around a square garden pond as follows:

pond 1   *pond 2*   *pond 3*   *pond 4*   *pond 5*

(i)   Write down the number pattern that he found.

(1 mark)

(ii)   How many slabs would be needed to pave around the 10th pond?

(1 mark)

(iii) What would be the nth term of this sequence?

(2 marks)

4 Jess is doing a mathematics investigation and obtained the results 1, 2, 4, 8, 16, 32.

(i)   What would be the next term in this sequence?

(1 mark)

(ii)   The 10th term?

(1 mark)

(iii) The nth term?

(2 marks)

5 Henry is investigating multilink staircases as follows:

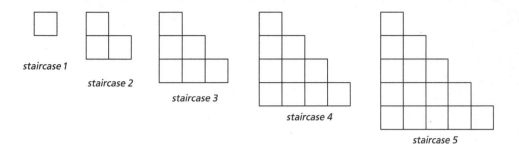

staircase 1

staircase 2

staircase 3

staircase 4

staircase 5

(i)   Write down the number pattern that he found.

(1 mark)

(ii)   How many cubes would be needed for the 10th staircase?

(1 mark)

(iii)   What would be the nth term of this sequence?

(2 marks)

Key vocabulary: *generalise, nth term, number sequence, equation, expression*

6 Solve the following equations:

(i) $\dfrac{1}{x+2} = 3$ (ii) $\dfrac{1}{5x-4} = \dfrac{1}{x}$

(iii) $\dfrac{3}{1+b} = \dfrac{5}{b+3}$

(3 marks)

Key vocabulary: *term, expression, equation*

7 Solve the following pairs of simultaneous equations:

(i) $\begin{cases} y - 2x = 4 \\ y + x = 7 \end{cases}$

(ii) $\begin{cases} 2a - 3b = 2 \\ 4a + 6b = 4 \end{cases}$

(iii) $\begin{cases} 2x - y = 5 \\ 3x + 2y = 11 \end{cases}$

(3 marks)

Key vocabulary: *simultaneous linear equation*

Shape and space

① If angle a is 100°, work out angles b, c, d, e and f.

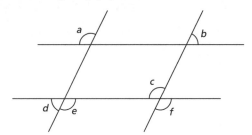

(1 mark)

② If angle $a = 95°$, angle $b = 110°$ and angle $c = 105°$, what does angle d equal?

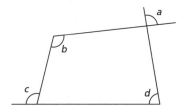

(1 mark)

Key vocabulary: *opposite angles, complementary angles, supplementary angles, interior angles*

③

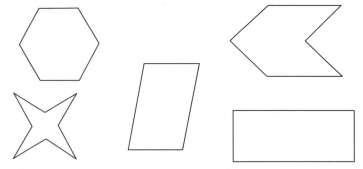

   (i)   Identify the lines of symmetry of the shapes above.

(5 marks)

   (ii) Identify the orders of rotational symmetry of the shapes above.

(5 marks)

Key vocabulary: *reflective symmetry, order of rotational symmetry*

4 Identify which of the angles in the following shape are acute, obtuse, right or reflex.

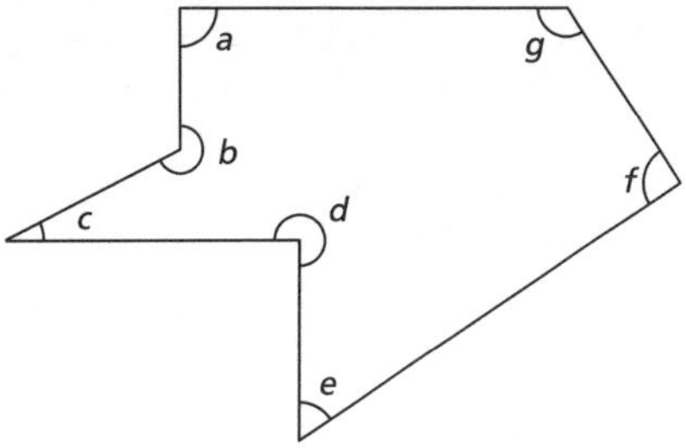

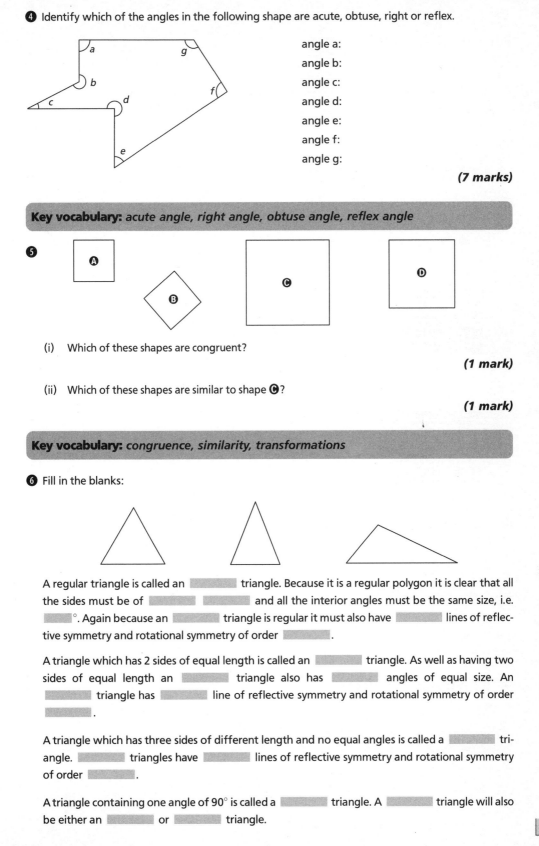

angle a:
angle b:
angle c:
angle d:
angle e:
angle f:
angle g:

(7 marks)

Key vocabulary: *acute angle, right angle, obtuse angle, reflex angle*

5

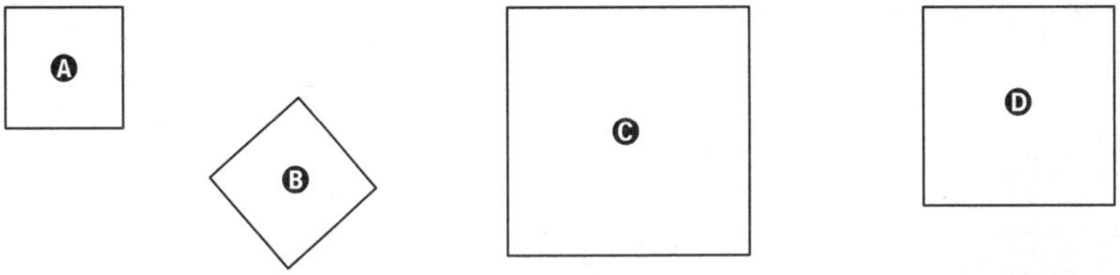

(i) Which of these shapes are congruent?

(1 mark)

(ii) Which of these shapes are similar to shape C?

(1 mark)

Key vocabulary: *congruence, similarity, transformations*

6 Fill in the blanks:

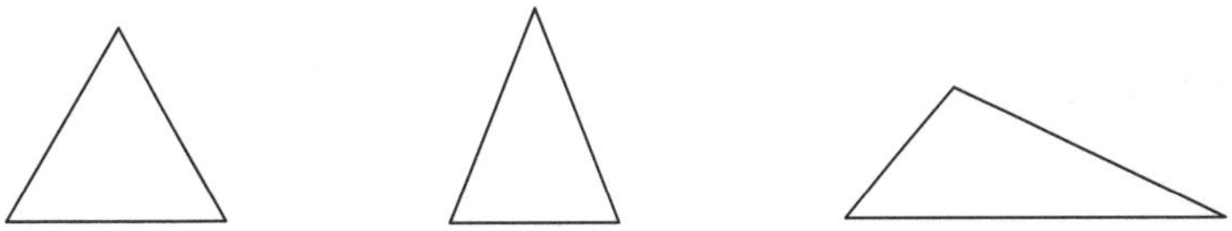

A regular triangle is called an ____ triangle. Because it is a regular polygon it is clear that all the sides must be of ____ ____ and all the interior angles must be the same size, i.e. ____°. Again because an ____ triangle is regular it must also have ____ lines of reflective symmetry and rotational symmetry of order ____.

A triangle which has 2 sides of equal length is called an ____ triangle. As well as having two sides of equal length an ____ triangle also has ____ angles of equal size. An ____ triangle has ____ line of reflective symmetry and rotational symmetry of order ____.

A triangle which has three sides of different length and no equal angles is called a ____ triangle. ____ triangles have ____ lines of reflective symmetry and rotational symmetry of order ____.

A triangle containing one angle of 90° is called a ____ triangle. A ____ triangle will also be either an ____ or ____ triangle.

The number of lines of reflective symmetry and the order of rotational symmetry of a ▨▨▨▨ triangle depends on whether it is an ▨▨▨▨ or ▨▨▨▨ triangle.

(24 marks)

Key vocabulary: *triangle, equilateral, isosceles, scalene, right-angled*

❼ Put a tick in the box if the following triangles have right angles:

(i)   AB = 3   BC = 4   AC = 5   ☐

(ii) XY = 4   YZ = 5   XZ = 6   ☐

(2 marks)

Key vocabulary: *Pythagoras' theorem, Pythagorean triples*

❽ What is the area of this triangle?

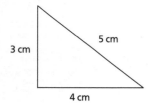

(1 mark)

❾ What is the area of this parallelogram?

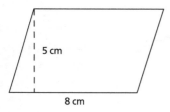

(1 mark)

❿ What is the area of this trapezium?

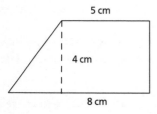

(1 mark)

⑪ Work out the perimeter and area of the following shape:

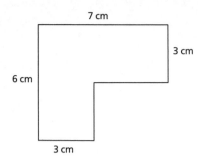

Perimeter =

Area =

(2 marks)

⑫ Work out the perimeter and area of the following shape (you will need to calculate a sensible value for *L*).

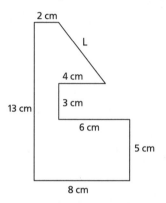

L =

Perimeter =

Area =

(3 marks)

Key vocabulary: *perimeter, area*

⑬ Find the circumference and area of a circle with a diameter of 10 cm.

(2 marks)

⑭

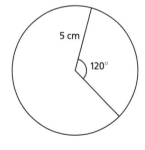

Circle A

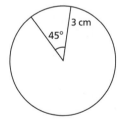

Circle B

(i) Calculate the area of the sector marked in each circle.

(2 marks)

(ii) Calculate the length of the arcs marked on each circle above.

(2 marks)

Key vocabulary: *radius, diameter, circumference, area, sector, arc*

⑮ This rectangle has the following coordinates:

a (1, 1)
b (1, 3)
c (5, 3)
d (5, 1)

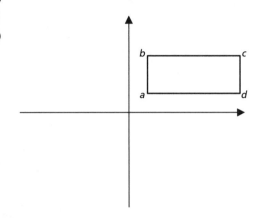

Work out the new coordinates when the rectangle is reflected in:

(i)   the y-axis
(ii) the line $x = y$

(2 marks)

Key vocabulary: *Cartesian coordinates, quadrant, abscissa, ordinate*

⑯ Name the *five* Platonic solids. What links the solids in this group?

(6 marks)

⑰ Draw *two* different nets for a tetrahedron.

(2 marks)

⑱ Draw three different nets for a cube.

(3 marks)

⑲ Identify the number of faces, vertices and edges on the following solids:

Solid	Faces	Edges	Vertices
Cube			
Tetrahedron			
Triangular prism			

(9 marks)

Key vocabulary: *face, edge, vertex, net*

⑳ A cuboid has edges of lengths 3 cm, 4 cm and 6 cm.

   (i)   What is the area of each face? *(3 marks)*
   (ii) What is the total surface area of the cuboid? *(1 mark)*
   (iii) What is the volume of the cuboid? *(1 mark)*

㉑ Find the surface area and volume of the following cylinder, with radius 5 cm and length 10 cm.

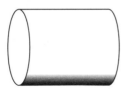

Surface area =

Volume =

(2 marks)

㉒ Find the surface area and volume of the following triangular prism:

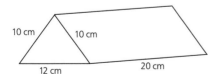

10 cm   10 cm

12 cm   20 cm

Surface area =

Volume =

(2 marks)

Key vocabulary: *surface area, volume*

Statistics

❶ The following tables show the results of a test taken by two classes. Inspect each of the sets of data and complete the table underneath.

Class A results

12	13	15	15	16	16	16	17	17	17
17	17	18	18	18	19	19	20	20	20

Class B results

10	11	8	11	14	17	15	12	19	11
18	20	17	19	16	11	20	17	15	19

	Class A data	Class B data
Mean		
Mode		
Median		
Range		

(8 marks)

❷ The wages of 10 workers in a factory are £30k, £22k, £6k, £6k, £6k, £6k, £6k, £6k, £6k, £6k. Find:

(i)   the mode
(ii) the mean
(iii) the median

If you were the union representative, which average would you use to justify a wage rise for the workers? Explain your reasoning.

(4 marks)

Key vocabulary: *mode, median, mean, range, discrete data, continuous data*

(Statistics _____ out of 12

Probability

❶ Dice are numbered 1–6. Two fair dice are thrown and the numbers added. Find the probability that the total is:

(i) 2   (ii) 7   (iii) 6   (iv) 14

(4 marks)

❷ (i)   A fair die is rolled. What is the probability that a 5 will be rolled?
   (ii) A coin is flipped. What is the probability of achieving tails?
   (iii) A fair die is rolled and a coin is flipped. What is the probability of achieving a 5 and tails?

(3 marks)

❸ A card is drawn from a pack of 52. What is the probability:

(i) it is a heart?

(ii) it is a black card?

(iii) it is a card less than a 10? (Ace is high)

(iv) that the card is higher than a Jack? (Ace is high)

(4 marks)

❹ Delyth has the following cards:

21 ☹	30 ☺	15 ☹	39 ☺	18 ☺	34 ☹	42 ☺	27 ☺

(i) Gareth takes a card without looking. He says, 'I'm more likely to have an even number than an odd number.' Is he correct? Explain.

(1 mark)

(ii) Choose one of the following words to complete the sentences below.

likely   impossible   certain   unlikely

(a) It is [_____] that Gareth's card will contain ☹

(b) It is [_____] that Gareth's number will be greater than 10.

(2 marks)

> **Key vocabulary:** *mutually exclusive, independent, tree diagram, outcome, relative frequency*

Measures

❶ What imperial and metric units could be used to measure the following:

	Imperial	Metric
Distance		
Speed		
Volume		
Capacity		
Mass		
Area		

(12 marks)

❷ James is following a recipe which is written using metric units of measurement.

   (i)   The recipe suggests using a mixing bowl with a diameter of 30 cm. How many inches should the diameter of the bowl be?

   (ii)   The recipe requires 1 litre of milk. How many pints must James use?

   (iii)   It also requires 500 g of flour. How many pounds and/or ounces are required?

                                                                          (3 marks)

❸ Put the following in size order, starting with the lightest:

   1 lb   250 g $\frac{1}{2}$ oz   1 kg $\frac{1}{2}$ lb   500 g   10 oz   25 g

                                                                          (1 mark)

❹ Put the following in size order, starting with the shortest:

   5.4 m   349 cm   16 m   2.4 km   1780 m   2567 m   1780 cm   5650 mm

                                                                          (1 mark)

Key vocabulary: *Imperial, metric, conversion*

Equations and graphs

❶ Amelia is setting out from home for a bike ride. The simplified graph shows the journey.

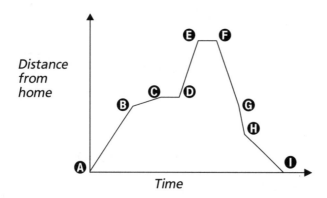

   (i)   Which part of the graph shows Amelia cycling up a steep hill?

                                                                          (1 mark)

   (ii)   Which parts of the graph show her having a rest?

                                                                          (2 marks)

   (iii)   Which point on the graph shows her arriving home?

                                                                          (1 mark)

❷ This is the graph of $y = 10x + 8$

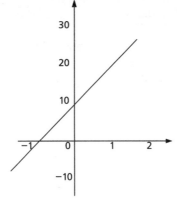

What is:

(i) the gradient of the line?

(ii) the y-intercept?

(2 marks)

❸ Write down the equation of the following graph:

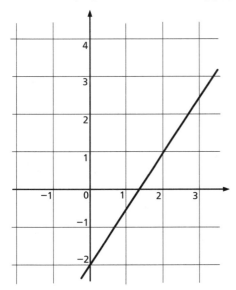

(1 mark)

❹ Write down the gradient and y-intercept of each of the following linear equations:

(i) $y = \frac{2}{3}x + 6$ Gradient =

            y-intercept =

(ii) $2y = 3x - 6$ Gradient =

            y-intercept =

(4 marks)

Key vocabulary: *gradient, y-intercept, linear*

Reasoning and proof

❶ Say whether the following statements are **true** or **false**. Explain your reasoning.

(i)   The product of two consecutive numbers is always divisible by 2. (The product of 3 and 4 is 12.)

(ii)   The sum of three consecutive numbers is always even

(iii) The product of three consecutive numbers is always divisible by 6

(3 marks)

❷ Which of the following are **true** and which are **false**? (x is a real number.)

(i) $2(x + 4) \equiv 2x + 8$

(ii) $3(x - 3) \equiv 3x - 6$

(iii) $x^2 = -4$

(3 marks)

❸ Prove that there are exactly four prime numbers between 10 and 20

(1 mark)

❹ Prove that the sum of any two odd numbers is even.

(1 mark)

❺ Show that when two six-faced dice are thrown a total of 6 is more likely than a total of 4.

(1 mark)

> **Key vocabulary:** *prove, show, deductive proof, proof by exhaustion, disproof by counter example, $\equiv$, $\therefore$, $\Rightarrow$)*

Making sense of your test results

How well did you do? Determine a separate % score for each area, and then determine an overall score for the test. Remember that your percentage score is relative to the nature of the material tested and the time at which the test took place.

	Score		Percentage
Number	*Marks*	*(max. 79)*	%
Algebra	*Marks*	*(max. 34)*	%
Shape and space	*Marks*	*(max. 92)*	%
Statistics	*Marks*	*(max. 12)*	%
Probability	*Marks*	*(max. 14)*	%
Measures	*Marks*	*(max. 17)*	%
Equations and graphs	*Marks*	*(max. 11)*	%
Reasoning and proof	*Marks*	*(max. 9)*	%
Overall	*Marks*	*(max. 268)*	%

Consider the following divisions against which your separate and overall test scores can be measured. The scale is based upon our experiences of testing trainees in this way. It should be used for guidance and to aid target setting and not taken as some sort of absolute test measure.

80–100%   In the areas tested, your score is very good and indicates that you probably exceed the level expected of a non-mathematics specialist. Well done.

60–80%   In the areas tested, your score is good and indicates that you probably meet the level expected of a non-mathematics specialist. Some attention is necessary in weaker questions. However, with these marks you probably have little to worry about.

50–60%   In the areas tested, your score is adequate and probably indicates that you are moving towards the level expected of a non-mathematics specialist. However, attention is necessary throughout. Just like the self-audit, you are probably in good company and with a little effort you'll be up there with the best of them.

0–50%   In the areas tested, your score is probably a bit on the low side. Use the test positively to target the areas you need to work on. Remember, you only have to get there by the end of your training. Your score wouldn't concern us at this stage, so don't let it concern you unduly.

A useful tip would be to take a break from testing for now. Use the test questions as a guide for some revision (see Part 7 for further recommendations). Come back to the different sections of the test later and see how much progress you have made.

Number

❶ (i) $45 \times 24 = 1080$

x	40	5	
20	800	100	900
4	160	20	180
			1080

(ii) $146 \times 234 = 34\,164$

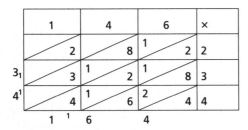

(iii) $312 \times 235 = 73\,320$

```
      312
  ×   235
     1560
     9360
    62400
    73320
    1 1 1
```

❷ (i) $1768 \div 34 = 52$

```
        52
  34)1768
      1700    (50 × 34)
        68
        68    (2 × 34)
         0
```

(ii) $1638 \div 63 = 26$

```
        26
  63)1638
     126
     378
     378
       0
```

(iii) $3335 \div 23 = 145$

```
       145
  23)3 3 3 5
       10  11
```

8 28
16 32
24 40 48 2

3 (i) $p + q = \frac{2}{3} + \frac{1}{2} = \frac{4}{6} + \frac{3}{6} = \frac{7}{6} = 1\frac{1}{6}$

(ii) $p + r = \frac{2}{3} + 2\frac{4}{7} = \frac{2}{3} + \frac{18}{7} = \frac{14}{21} + \frac{54}{21} = \frac{68}{21} = 3\frac{5}{21}$

(iii) $q + s = \frac{1}{2} + 1\frac{1}{5} = \frac{1}{2} + \frac{6}{5} = \frac{5}{10} + \frac{12}{10} = \frac{17}{10} = 1\frac{7}{10}$

(iv) $p - q = \frac{2}{3} - \frac{1}{2} = \frac{4}{6} - \frac{3}{6} = \frac{1}{6}$

(v) $r - q = 2\frac{4}{7} - \frac{1}{2} = \frac{18}{7} - \frac{1}{2} = \frac{36}{14} - \frac{7}{14} = \frac{29}{14} = 2\frac{1}{14}$

(vi) $r - s = 2\frac{4}{7} - 1\frac{1}{5} = \frac{18}{7} - \frac{6}{5} = \frac{90}{35} - \frac{42}{35} = \frac{48}{35} = 1\frac{13}{35}$

(vii) $p \times q = \frac{2}{3} \times \frac{1}{2} = \frac{2}{6} = \frac{1}{3}$

(viii) $q \times s = \frac{1}{2} \times 1\frac{1}{5} = \frac{1}{2} \times \frac{6}{5} = \frac{6}{10} = \frac{3}{5}$

(ix) $r \times s = 2\frac{4}{7} \times 1\frac{1}{5} = \frac{18}{7} \times \frac{6}{5} = \frac{108}{35} = 3\frac{3}{35}$

(x) $p \div q = \frac{2}{3} \div \frac{1}{2} = \frac{2}{3} \times \frac{2}{1} = \frac{4}{3} = 1\frac{1}{3}$

(xi) $q \div p = \frac{1}{2} \div \frac{2}{3} = \frac{1}{2} \times \frac{3}{2} = \frac{3}{4}$

(xii) $q \div r = \frac{1}{2} \div 2\frac{4}{7} = \frac{1}{2} \times \frac{7}{18} = \frac{7}{36}$

4 (i) $\frac{5}{8} = 0.625$

$$\begin{array}{r} 0.625 \\ 8 \overline{)5.^50^00} \end{array}$$

(ii) $\frac{7}{20} = 0.35$

$$\begin{array}{r} 0.35 \\ 20 \overline{)7.^70^00} \end{array}$$

(iii) $65\% = 0.65$

(iv) $0.1\% = 0.001$

5 (i) $0.375 = \frac{375}{1000} = \frac{3}{8}$

(ii) $0.28 = \frac{28}{100} = \frac{14}{50} = \frac{7}{25}$

(iii) $76\% = \frac{76}{100} = \frac{38}{50} = \frac{19}{25}$

6 (i) $\frac{84}{96} = \frac{42}{48} = \frac{21}{24} = \frac{7}{8}$

(ii) $\frac{84}{91} = \frac{12}{13}$

7 (i) $\frac{5}{8} = 0.625 = 62.5\%$

(ii) $0.375 = 37.5\%$

(iii) $\frac{7}{20} = 0.35 = 35\%$

(iv) $0.28 = 28\%$

8 4% cheaper:

Let the original price be n

A 20% increase is equal to $0.2n$

So the pre-Christmas price is $n + 0.2n = 1.2n$

A post-Christmas 20% decrease is equal to $0.24n$

So the post-Christmas price is $1.2n - 0.24n = 0.96n$

The percentage decrease from n to $0.96n$ is 4%

Hence the game is only 4% cheaper.

9 The two prices are the same:

Let the original price be n

A 25% increase is equal to $0.25n$

So the increased price is $n + 0.25n = 1.25n$

The 20% reduction is equal to $0.25n$

So the reduced price is $1.25n - 0.25n = n$

Hence the reduced price is equal to the original price.

10 In the first game the team scored 24 points; in the second game they scored 30 points. There was an increase of 6 points from the first game to the second game. As a percentage this increase can be represented as $\frac{6}{24} \times 100\% = 25\%$.

11 For every £5 raised Edward contributed £2 (i.e. $\frac{2}{5}$) and Katherine contributed £3 (i.e. $\frac{3}{5}$). Applying this to the £160 total raised gives:

Edward: $\frac{2}{5}$ x £160 = £64

Katherine: $\frac{3}{5}$ x £160 = £96

12 This is the same type of problem as question 11, only slightly larger.

The books are shared in the ratio 52 (i.e. $\frac{52}{200}$) to 68 (i.e. $\frac{68}{200}$) to 44 (i.e. $\frac{44}{200}$) to 36 (i.e. $\frac{36}{200}$). Applying this to the 1000 books to be distributed gives:

Year 3: $\frac{52}{200} \times 1000$ books = 260 books

Year 4: $\frac{68}{200} \times 1000$ books = 340 books

Year 5: $\frac{44}{200} \times 1000$ books = 220 books

Year 6: $\frac{36}{200} \times 1000$ books = 180 books

13 (i) ☑   (ii) ☒   (iii) ☑

(iv) ☒   (v) ☑   (vi) ☑

(vii) ☒   (viii) ☑   (ix) ☑

14 $-(2^2)$ $-\sqrt{5}$ $-(2^{-2})$ $0.1010010001...$ $\frac{1}{9}$ 2^{-3} $\frac{1}{7}$

    $0.\dot{3}$ 0.363636 $\sqrt{\frac{4}{9}}$ $\sqrt{2}$ $\sqrt{4}$ π 2^3

15 (i) $0.2\dot{7}$ (ii) $0.\dot{2}\dot{7}$ (iii) $0.90\dot{4}$ (iv) $18.\dot{1}\dot{8}$

16 (i) $100\,000 = 10^5$ (ii) $0.1 = 10^{-1}$ (iii) $100 = 10^2$

17 (i) $6.6 \times 10^3 = 6600$ (ii) $7.07 \times 10^{-2} = 0.0707$

18 (i) $523\,000 = 5.23 \times 10^5$ (ii) $0.0606 = 6.06 \times 10^{-2}$

19 (i) ☑   (ii) ☒   (iii) ☑   (iv) ☒

20 (i) Factors of 18: 1, 2, 3, 6, 9, 18

(ii) Factors of 60: 1, 2, 3, 4, 5, 6, 10, 12, 15, 20, 30, 60

21 (i) Factors of 48: 1, 2, 3, 4, 6, 8, 12, 16, 24, 48

Of these only 2 and 3 are prime, hence these are the prime factors.

(ii) Factors of 105: 1, 3, 5, 7, 15, 21, 35, 105

Of these only 3, 5 and 7 are prime, hence these are the prime factors.

22 (i) Factors of 6: 1, 2, 3, 6

Factors of 15: 1, 3, 5, 15

1 and 3 are factors common to both 6 and 15.

3 is the highest common factor.

(ii) Factors of 18: 1, 2, 3, 6, 9, 18

Factors of 54: 1, 2, 3, 6, 9, 18, 27, 54

1, 2, 3, 6, 9 and 18 are factors common to both 18 and 54.

18 is the highest common factor.

(iii) Factors of $12a^2$: 1, 2, 3, 4, 6, 12, a, $2a$, $3a$, $4a$, $6a$, $12a$, a^2, $2a^2$, $3a^2$, $4a^2$, $6a^2$, $12a^2$

Factors of $4ab$: 1, 2, 4, a, $2a$, $4a$, b, $2b$, $4b$, ab, $2ab$, $4ab$

1, 2, 4, a, $2a$ and $4a$ are factors common to both $12a^2$ and $4ab$.

$4a$ is the highest common factor.

(iv) Factors of a^2b: 1, a, a^2, b, ab, a^2b

Factors of a^3b^2: 1, a, a^2, a^3, b, b^2, ab, a^2b, a^3b, ab^2, a^2b^2, a^3b^2

1, a, a^2, b, ab, a^2b are factors common to both a^2b and a^3b^2.

a^2b is the highest common factor.

Algebra – Patterns and relationships

1 (i) $ab = 5 \times 15 = 75$

(ii) $ac = 5 \times 2 = 10$

(iii) $de = 15$ and $d = 3$, hence $e = 15 \div 3 = 5$

(iv) $df = 18$ and $d = 3$, hence $f = 18 \div 3 = 6$

(v) $a(b + c) = 5(15 + 2) = 85$

(vi) $d(e + f) = 3(5 + 6) = 33$

(vii) $a(b - c) = 5(15 - 2) = 65$

(viii) $d(e - f) = 3(5 - 6) = -3$

(ix) $2a^2b = 2 \times 5^2 \times 15 = 750$

(x) $2d^2e = 2 \times 3^2 \times 5 = 90$

(xi) $\frac{1}{a} = \frac{1}{5}$ or 0.2

(xii) $\frac{1}{d} = \frac{1}{3}$ or 0.333

2 (i) 36

(ii) 100

(iii) n^2

3 (i) 8, 12, 16, 20, 24

(ii) 44 slabs

(iii) $4n + 4 = 4(n + 1)$

4 (i) 64

(ii) 512

(iii) $2^{(n-1)}$

5 (i) 1, 3, 6, 10, 15

(ii) 55 cubes

(iii) $\dfrac{n(n + 1)}{2}$

6 (i)

$$\frac{1}{x+2} = 3$$

$$1 = 3(x+2)$$
$$1 = 3x + 6$$
$$-5 = 3x$$
$$x = \frac{-5}{3}$$

(ii)

$$\frac{1}{5x-4} = \frac{1}{x}$$

$$x = 5x - 4$$
$$4 = 4x$$
$$x = 1$$

(iii)

$$\frac{3}{1+b} = \frac{5}{b+3}$$

$$3(b+3) = 5(1+b)$$
$$3b + 9 = 5 + 5b$$
$$4 = 2b$$
$$2 = b$$

7 (i) $\begin{cases} y - 2x = 4 \ (1) \\ y + x = 7 \ (2) \end{cases}$

(2) − (1):
$$y + x = 7$$
$$- \ \underline{y - 2x = 4}$$
$$3x = 3$$
$$x = 1$$

Substitute in (2):
$$y + x = 7$$
$$y + 1 = 7$$
$$y = 6$$

(ii) $\begin{cases} 2a - 3b = 2 \ (1) \\ 4a + 6b = 4 \ (2) \end{cases}$

rearranging (1) gives:

$$a = \frac{2 + 3b}{2}$$

Substituting for a in (2) gives:

$$4a + 6b = 4$$

$$4\left(\frac{2 + 3b}{2}\right) + 6b = 4$$

$$4 + 6b + 6b = 4$$
$$12b = 0$$
$$b = 0$$

Substituting for b in (1) gives:

$$2a - 3b = 2$$
$$2a - 0 = 2$$
$$a = 1$$

(iii) $\begin{cases} 2x - y = 5 \\ 3x + 2y = 11 \end{cases}$

By drawing the graphs represented by the two equations it is possible to find the common solution. The common solution is found where the two lines cross. At this point the values for x and y in both of the equations are the same.

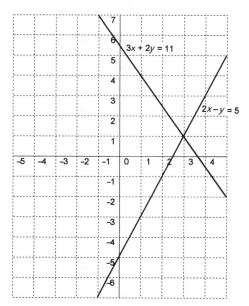

In this case the lines cross at the point (3,1), giving the common solution:

$x = 3$ and
$y = 1$

Shape and space

 1 $b = 80°$ $c = 100°$ $d = 80°$ $e = 100°$ $f = 100°$

2 angle $d = 80°$

3

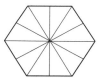

6 lines of reflective symmetry
rotational symmetry of order 6

no lines of reflective symmetry
rotational symmetry of order 2

1 line of reflective symmetry
rotational symmetry of order 1

4 lines of reflective symmetry
rotational symmetry of order 4

2 lines of reflective symmetry
rotational symmetry of order 2

④   angle a: right   angle b: reflex   angle c: acute   angle d: reflex

      angle e: acute   angle f: right   angle g: obtuse

⑤ (i)   shapes Ⓐ and Ⓑ are congruent

    (ii)   all of the other shapes, Ⓐ, Ⓑ and Ⓓ are similar to shape Ⓒ

⑥ A regular triangle is called an **equilateral** triangle. Because it is a regular polygon it is clear that all the sides must be of **equal length** and all the interior angles must be the same size, i.e. **60°**. Again because an **equilateral** triangle is regular it must also have **three** lines of reflective symmetry and rotational symmetry of order **3**.

A triangle which has two sides of equal length is called an **isosceles** triangle. As well as having two sides of equal length an **isosceles** triangle also has **two** angles of equal size. An **isosceles** triangle has **one** line of reflective symmetry and rotational symmetry of order **1**.

A triangle which has three sides of different length and no equal angles is called a **scalene** triangle. **Scalene** triangles have **no** lines of reflective symmetry and rotational symmetry of order **1**.

A triangle containing one angle of 90° is called a **right-angled** triangle. A **right-angled** triangle will also be either an **isosceles** or **scalene** triangle.

The number of lines of reflective symmetry and the order of rotational symmetry of a **right-angled** triangle depends on whether it is an **isosceles** or **scalene** triangle.

⑦ Right-angled triangles satisfy Pythagoras' theorem, i.e. $a^2 + b^2 = c^2$

(i) $3^2 + 4^2 = 5^2$, hence the triangle has a right angle

(ii) $4^2 + 5^2 = 41$ not 6^2, hence the triangle does not have a right angle

⑧ Area of the triangle is equal to half × base × height = 2 cm × 3 cm = 6cm^2

⑨ Area of the parallelogram is equal to base × height = 8 cm × 5 cm = 40 cm^2

⑩ Area of the trapezium is found by dissecting it into a parallelogram and a triangle, then adding the area of the parallelogram and the area of the triangle:

$$\text{Area of parallelogram + Area of triangle} = (5 \text{ cm} \times 4 \text{ cm}) + (1.5 \text{ cm} \times 4 \text{ cm})$$
$$= 20 \text{ cm}^2 + 6 \text{ cm}^2$$
$$= 26 \text{ cm}^2$$

⑪   Perimeter $= 7 \text{ cm} + 3 \text{ cm} + 3 \text{ cm} + 6 \text{ cm} + (7 - 3) \text{ cm} + (6 - 3) \text{ cm}$

                $= 7 \text{ cm} + 3 \text{ cm} + 3 \text{ cm} + 6 \text{ cm} + 4 \text{ cm} + 3 \text{ cm}$

                $= 26 \text{ cm}$

        Area $= (7 \times 6) \text{ cm}^2 - (4 \times 3) \text{ cm}^2$

              $= 42 \text{ cm}^2 - 12 \text{ cm}^2$

              $= 30 \text{ cm}^2$

⑫ Using Pythagoras' theorem to calculate L:

$$4^2 + 5^2 = L^2$$
$$16 + 25 = L^2$$
$$41 = L^2$$
$$\sqrt{41} = L$$
$$L \approx 6.4 \text{ cm}$$

Perimeter $\approx$ 2 cm + 13 cm + 8 cm + 5 cm + 6 cm + 3 cm + 4 cm + 6.4 cm

$\approx$ 47.4 cm

Area $= (2 \times 13) \text{ cm}^2 + (6 \times 5) \text{ cm}^2 + (\frac{1}{2} \times 4 \times 5) \text{ cm}^2$

$= 26 \text{ cm}^2 + 30 \text{ cm}^2 + 10 \text{ cm}^2$
$= 66 \text{ cm}^2$

⑬ Circumference $= \pi d$

$= 10\pi \text{ cm}$

$\approx$ 31.4 cm   (taking π to be 3.14)

Area $= \pi r^2$

$= 25\pi \text{ cm}^2$

$\approx$ 78.5 cm^2 (taking π to be 3.14)

⑭ (i) Area of circle Ⓐ $= \pi r^2$

$= 25\pi \text{ cm}^2$

$\approx$ 78.5 cm^2

The sector marked in circle Ⓐ represents $\frac{1}{3}$ of the circle because 120° is $\frac{1}{3}$ of 360°. Hence the area of the sector in circle Ⓐ is $\frac{1}{3} \times 78.5 \text{ cm}^2 = 26.17 \text{ cm}^2$

Area of circle Ⓑ $= \pi r^2$

$= 9\pi \text{ cm}^2$

$\approx$ 28.26 cm^2

The sector marked in circle Ⓑ represents $\frac{1}{8}$ of the circle because 45° is $\frac{1}{8}$ of 360°. Hence the area of the sector in circle Ⓑ is $\frac{1}{8} \times 28.26 \text{ cm}^2 = 3.53 \text{ cm}^2$

(ii) The circumference of circle Ⓐ $= 2\pi r$

$= 10\pi \text{ cm}$

$\approx$ 31.4 cm

The length of the arc marked in circle Ⓐ represents $\frac{1}{3}$ the length of the circumference because 120° is $\frac{1}{3}$ of 360°.

Hence the length of the arc in circle Ⓐ is $\frac{1}{3} \times 31.4 \text{ cm} = 10.47 \text{ cm}$

The circumference of circle Ⓑ $= 2\pi r$

$= 6\pi \text{ cm}$

$\approx$ 18.84 cm

The length of the arc marked in circle Ⓑ represents $\frac{1}{8}$ the length of the circumference because 45° is $\frac{1}{8}$ of 360°.

Hence the length of the arc in circle Ⓑ is $\frac{1}{8} \times 18.84 \text{ cm} = 2.36 \text{ cm}$

15 (i) Reflection in the *y*-axis has the effect of multiplying the *x*-coordinate (or abscissa) by −1, giving:

$a' = (-1, 1)$
$b' = (-1, 3)$
$c' = (-5, 3)$
$d' = (-5, 1)$

(ii) Reflection in the line $x = y$ has the effect of exchanging the *x* and *y* coordinates (abscissa and ordinate), giving:

$a'' = (1, 1)$
$b'' = (3, 1)$
$c'' = (3, 5)$
$d'' = (1, 5)$

16 The five Platonic solids are:

- **regular tetrahedron**
- **cube**
- **regular octahedron**
- **regular dodecahedron**
- **regular icosahedron**

The Platonic solids are the only regular solids. A polyhedron is defined as regular if all faces are congruent and all the angles between the faces (i.e. the dihedral angles) are the same size.

17

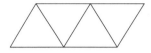 

18

⑲

Solid	Faces	Edges	Vertices
Cube	6	12	8
Tetrahedron	4	6	4
Triangular prism	5	9	6

⑳ (i) The cuboid has:

2 faces with an area of 3 cm × 4 cm = 12 cm^2
2 faces with an area of 4 cm × 6 cm = 24 cm^2
2 faces with an area of 3 cm × 6 cm = 18 cm^2

(ii) The total surface area = (2 × 12 cm^2) + (2 × 24 cm^2) + (2 × 18 cm^2)
$\qquad\qquad\qquad\qquad$ = 24 cm^2 + 48 cm^2 + 36 cm^2
$\qquad\qquad\qquad\qquad$ = 108 cm^2

(iii) The volume of the cuboid = 3 cm × 4 cm × 6 cm
$\qquad\qquad\qquad\qquad\qquad$ = 72 cm^3

㉑ Surface area:

Area of each circular face = πr^2
$\qquad\qquad\qquad\qquad$ = 25π cm^2
$\qquad\qquad\qquad\qquad$ ≈ 78.5 cm^2

Area of curved surface = 10 × 2πr cm^2
$\qquad\qquad\qquad\qquad$ = 10 × 10π cm^2
$\qquad\qquad\qquad\qquad$ ≈ 314 cm^2

Total surface area = (2 × 78.5 cm^2) + 314 cm^2
$\qquad\qquad\qquad$ = 157 cm^2 + 314 cm^2
$\qquad\qquad\qquad$ = 471 cm^2

Volume:

Area of circular face × length = 78.5 cm^2 × 10 cm
$\qquad\qquad\qquad\qquad\qquad$ = 785 cm^3

㉒ Surface area:

Area of each triangular face = 6 cm × 8 cm
$\qquad\qquad\qquad\qquad\qquad$ = 48 cm^2

Area of 2 rectangular faces = 10 cm × 20 cm
$\qquad\qquad\qquad\qquad\qquad$ = 200 cm^2

Area of remaining rectangular face = 12 cm × 20 cm
$\qquad\qquad\qquad\qquad\qquad\qquad$ = 240 cm^2

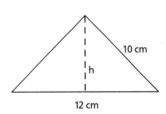

12 cm

Total surface area = (2 × 48 cm^2) + (2 × 200 cm^2) + 240 cm^2
$\qquad\qquad\qquad$ = 96 cm^2 + 400 cm^2 + 240 cm^2
$\qquad\qquad\qquad$ = 736 cm^2

Using Pythagoras $10^2 = 6^2 + h^2$
$\qquad\qquad\qquad 10^2 - 6^2 = h^2$
$\qquad\qquad\qquad 100 - 36 = h^2$
$\qquad\qquad\qquad\qquad 64 = h^2$
$\qquad\qquad\qquad\qquad h = 8$ cm

Volume:

Area of triangular face × length = 48 cm^2 × 20 cm
$\qquad\qquad\qquad\qquad\qquad\qquad$ = 960 cm^3

Statistics

❶

	Class A data	Class B data
Mean	17	15
Mode	17	11
Median	17	15.5
Range	8	12

❷ (i) mode = £6k

(ii) mean = £10k

(iii) median = £6k

Either the mode or the median would be an appropriate average to justify a wage increase.

Probability

❶ (i) $\frac{1}{36}$ (ii) $\frac{6}{36} = \frac{1}{6}$ (iii) $\frac{5}{36}$ (iv) 0

❷ (i) $\frac{1}{6}$ (ii) $\frac{1}{2}$ (iii) $\frac{1}{6} \times \frac{1}{2} = \frac{1}{12}$

❸ (i) $\frac{13}{52} = \frac{1}{4}$ (ii) $\frac{26}{52} = \frac{1}{2}$ (iii) $\frac{32}{52} = \frac{16}{26} = \frac{8}{13}$ (iv) $\frac{12}{52} = \frac{6}{26} = \frac{3}{13}$

❹ (i) He is not correct. There is an equal number of even and odd cards, therefore it is equally likely that he will have an even number or an odd number.

(ii) (a) unlikely
(b) certain

Measures

❶

	Imperial	Metric
Distance	mile	km
Speed	mph	kmh^{-1}
Volume	cubic foot	m^3
Capacity	pint	litre
Mass	lb	kg
Area	square foot	m^2

❷ (i) taking approx. 2.5 cm to the inch gives 12 inches

(ii) appox. 1.75 pints

(iii) approx 2.2 pounds to the kilogram, hence 1.1 pounds in 500 g. 1.1 pounds is about 1 lb $1\frac{1}{2}$ oz.

3 $\frac{1}{2}$ oz   25 g $\frac{1}{2}$ lb   250 g   10 oz   1 lb   500 g   1 kg

4 349 cm   5.4 m   5650 mm   16 m   1780 cm   1780 m   2.4 km   2567 m

Equations and graphs

1 (i) B – C   (ii) C – D and E – F   (iii) I

2 Using $y = mx + c$ as the general equation of a straight line, where m is the gradient and c is the y-intercept gives:

   (i)   gradient = 10

   (ii) y-intercept = 8

3 Using $y = mx + c$

   m = gradient $c = y$-intercept

     $= \frac{3}{2}$ $= -2$

   Substituting into the general equation gives:

   $y = \frac{3}{2}x - 2$

4 (i)   gradient $= \frac{2}{3}$ y-intercept = 6

   (ii) gradient $= \frac{3}{2}$ y-intercept = -3

Reasoning and proof

1 (i)   **True** – The product of an odd number multiplied by an even number always gives an even number. As one of the two numbers is even, it has a factor of 2; hence the product will have a factor of 2.

   (ii) **False** – This can be shown using disproof by counter example:

        Let the three consecutive numbers be 2, 3, 4

        Summing gives 2 + 3 + 4 = 9

        This is not even, hence the statement is false.

   (iii) **True** – The product of three consecutive numbers is always divisible by 6. Within any three consecutive numbers one must be even and therefore have a factor of 2, and one must have a factor of 3. Hence the product will have a factor of 2 × 3, i.e. 6.

2 (i) **True**   (ii) **False**   (iii) **False**

3 Consider the factors of all the numbers from 10 to 20:

      10 has factors: 1, 2, 5, 10   11 has factors: 1, 11

      12 has factors: 1, 2, 3, 4, 6, 12   13 has factors: 1, 13

      14 has factors: 1, 2, 7, 14   15 has factors: 1, 3, 5, 15

      16 has factors: 1, 2, 4, 8, 16   17 has factors: 1, 17

      18 has factors: 1, 2, 3, 6, 9, 18   19 has factors: 1, 19

      20 has factors: 1, 2, 4, 5, 10, 20

   This method of proof by exhaustion shows that there are exactly four prime numbers between 10 and 20: 11, 13, 17, 19.

4 Let the two odd numbers be $2a + 1$ and $2b + 1$ (where a and b are both integers)

Adding gives $(2a + 1) + (2b + 1) = 2a + 2b + 2$
$$= 2(a + b + 1)$$

$a + b + 1$ is an integer, which implies that $2(a + b + 1)$ is even

5 A table can be used to show all the possible outcomes:

Die 1	Die 2	Total	Die 1	Die 2	Total	Die 1	Die 2	Total	Die 1	Die 2	Total	Die 1	Die 2	Total	Die 1	Die 2	Total
1	1	2	2	1	3	3	1	4	4	1	5	5	1	6	6	1	7
1	2	3	2	2	4	3	2	5	4	2	6	5	2	7	6	2	8
1	3	4	2	3	5	3	3	6	4	3	7	5	3	8	6	3	9
1	4	5	2	4	6	3	4	7	4	4	8	5	4	9	6	4	10
1	5	6	2	5	7	3	5	8	4	5	9	5	5	10	6	5	11
1	6	7	2	6	8	3	6	9	4	6	10	5	6	11	6	6	12

From the table it can be seen that when throwing two dice the probability of obtaining a 6 is $\frac{5}{36}$ and the probability of obtaining a 4 is $\frac{3}{36}$, which shows that 6 is a more likely outcome than 4.

Teachers are constantly engaged in target setting, for example when assessing and marking children's work, when keeping records and when evaluating their own performance. Target setting is seen as a positive step towards ensuring progress and raising attainment. As your own training gets under way, you might well be asked to set targets for yourself. Targets will almost certainly be set for you!

Formally record your targets for further development below. Make **clear** and **specific** reference to areas within your self-audit and mathematics test that require attention. Don't forget to indicate where, when and how the targets will be achieved.

targets
(areas identified from the audit and test results requiring attention)

Number	Algebra – patterns and relationships	Shape and space

Statistics	Probability	Measures

Equations and graphs	Reasoning and proof	

Well done indeed for getting this far! By working through this book you are well on your way towards developing your mathematical knowledge and understanding. Having set targets it is useful to know where to go for further subject knowledge support. This section outlines some of the possible choices.

There are many books to support the development of mathematical knowledge currently available. As a trainee teacher it is probably more appropriate to look at books written specifically to address the mathematical needs of trainees. Various books have been written to support students as they work to develop their subject knowledge. Some books look solely at subject knowledge, others attempt to place it more firmly within a classroom context. It depends on your own needs when developing your subject knowledge, as to which of these is most appropriate for you. One book which addresses the learning within a classroom context is detailed below.

- Mooney, C. et al. (2002) *Primary Mathematics: Knowledge and Understanding* (second edition). Exeter: Learning Matters.

  The approach this book adopts endeavours to tackle the subject knowledge through a series of misconceptions that children may demonstrate in the classroom. The subject knowledge required by the teacher to effectively support and extend the child is then detailed. It also includes a review of research in each of the areas, as well as self-assessment questions to check understanding.

It is also possible to buy plenty of GCSE revision texts which help develop knowledge at a similar level to that required by trainees. However, if you are just seeking to improve your knowledge in the areas outlined within this text, then a potential problem using these books could be that the knowledge covered is not necessarily the knowledge required. In some areas it may be wider, in others more limited. If you are a little uncertain about mathematics, the format and the level might be a little intimidating. If you are more confident and just a little 'rusty' in a few areas they might be a suitable option.

A further option is to use the Internet to support your learning. Including specific website addresses in a book is rather risky as they tend to change quite regularly. Included here are a couple which are well established and were current at the time of writing.

- For help with revision at GCSE level, the BBC's Bitesize site is quite useful:

  http://www.bbc.co.uk/education/gcsebitesize/maths/index.shtml

- Considering mathematics more broadly, the Math Forum home page is a useful starting point. From here it is possible to search their Internet mathematics library for useful pages related to an incredibly diverse number of mathematical topics. It is also possible to e-mail Dr. Math with their Ask Dr. Math facility. Using this, any mathematical questions you have can be e-mailed to the Forum, who will endeavour to answer your question and publish the answer on the site.

  http://mathforum.com/

Also, remember that study groups with other trainees can be invaluable. Choosing the most appropriate resource for your needs, setting clear, achievable targets and identifying specific time to develop your mathematical knowledge, skills and understanding will all support you as you work towards achieving all the requirements for gaining QTS and becoming a confident and successful teacher.

Achieving QTS

Our *Achieving QTS* series now includes nearly 20 titles, encompassing *Audit and Test*, *Knowledge and Understanding*, *Teaching Theory and Practice*, and *Skills Tests* titles. As well as covering the core primary subject areas, the series addresses issues of teaching and learning across both primary and secondary phases. The Teacher Training Agency has identified books in this series as high quality resources for trainee teachers. You can find general information on each of these ranges on our website: www.learningmatters.co.uk

Primary English
Audit and Test (second edition)
Doreen Challen
£8   64 pages   ISBN: 1 903300 86 X

Primary Mathematics
Audit and Test (second edition)
Claire Mooney and Mike Fletcher
£8   52 pages   ISBN: 1 903300 87 8

Primary Science
Audit and Test (second edition)
John Sharp and Jenny Byrne
£8   80 pages   ISBN: 1 903300 88 6

Primary English
Knowledge and Understanding (second edition)
Jane Medwell, George Moore, David Wray, Vivienne Griffiths
£15   224 pages   ISBN: 1 903300 53 3

Primary English
Teaching Theory and Practice (second edition)
Jane Medwell, David Wray, Hilary Minns, Vivienne Griffiths, Elizabeth Coates
£15   192 pages   ISBN: 1 903300 54 1

Primary Mathematics
Knowledge and Understanding (second edition)
Claire Mooney, Lindsey Ferrie, Sue Fox, Alice Hansen, Reg Wrathmell
£15   176 pages   ISBN: 1 903300 55 X

Primary Mathematics
Teaching Theory and Practice (second edition)
Claire Mooney, Mary Briggs, Mike Fletcher, Judith McCullouch
£15   192 pages   ISBN: 1 903300 56 8

Primary Science
Knowledge and Understanding (second edition)
Rob Johnsey, Graham Peacock, John Sharp, Debbie Wright
£15   224 pages   ISBN: 1 903300 57 6

Primary Science
Teaching Theory and Practice (second edition)
John Sharp, Graham Peacock, Rob Johnsey, Shirley Simon, Robin Smith
£15   144 pages   ISBN: 1 903300 58 4

Primary ICT
Knowledge, Understanding and Practice (second edition)
Jane Sharp, John Potter, Jonathan Allen, Avril Loveless
£15   256 pages   ISBN: 1 903300 59 2

Professional Studies
Primary Phase (second edition)
Edited by Kate Jacques and Rob Hyland
£15   224 pages   ISBN: 1 903300 60 6

Teaching Foundation Stage
Edited by Iris Keating
£15   192 pages   ISBN: 1 903300 33 9

Teaching Humanities in Primary Schools
Pat Hoodless, Sue Bermingham, Elaine McReery, Paul Bowen
£15   192 pages   ISBN: 1 903300 36 3

Teaching Arts in Primary Schools
Stephanie Penny, Raywen Ford, Lawry Price, Susan Young
£15   192 pages   ISBN: 1 903300 35 5

Learning and Teaching in Secondary Schools
Edited by Viv Ellis
£15   192 pages   ISBN: 1 903300 38 X

Passing the Numeracy Skills Test (third edition)
Mark Patmore
£8   64 pages   ISBN: 1 903300 94 0

Passing the Literacy Skills Test
Jim Johnson
£6.99   80 pages   ISBN: 1 903300 12 6

Passing the ICT Skills Test
Clive Ferrigan
£6.99   80 pages   ISBN: 1 903300 13 4

Succeeding in the Induction Year (third edition)
Neil Simco
£13   144 pages   ISBN: 1 903300 93 2

To order, please contact:

Learning Matters Ltd
33 Southernhay East
Exeter EX1 1NX

Tel: 0845 230 9000
Fax: 01392 215 561
Email: orders@learningmatters.co.uk